Audio Access Included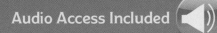

BLUES HARMONICA
BENDING & BEYOND

By Steve Cohen

PLAYBACK+
Speed • Pitch • Balance • Loop

To access audio visit:
www.halleonard.com/mylibrary

Enter Code
6988-5657-2558-0070

All harmonica and guitar played by Steve Cohen

Steve Cohen can be found through his website
www.stevecohenblues.com

ISBN 978-1-5400-1362-0

Visit Hal Leonard Online at
www.halleonard.com

Contact us:
Hal Leonard
7777 West Bluemound Road
Milwaukee, WI 53213
Email: info@halleonard.com

In Europe, contact:
Hal Leonard Europe Limited
42 Wigmore Street
Marylebone, London, W1U 2RN
Email: info@halleonardeurope.com

In Australia, contact:
Hal Leonard Australia Pty. Ltd.
4 Lentara Court
Cheltenham, Victoria, 3192 Australia
Email: info@halleonard.com.au

CONTENTS

INTRODUCTION

It is pretty easy to get a decent, in-tune sound out of a 10-hole diatonic harmonica. The reeds are structured in an easy-to-understand pattern, and one needs only to master some rudimentary skills to get started. Just by breathing in and out, you can play some nice sounding musical chords. Learning to isolate individual notes is one of the first basic skills needed to move to the next level, which is the ability to play single-note melodies.

The harmonica has some unique features. One is that notes are played by both inhaling (drawing) and exhaling (blowing). This is unique in the world of musical instruments.

It should also be noted that all of the action on a harmonica is hidden. You can't see the apparatus that makes the music, such as fingers on frets, or piano or saxophone keys, and you can't watch the reeds vibrate while music is being made. So rather than a visual approach to learning, a more intuitive approach involving muscle memory and familiarity through practice is essential.

As the beginner tries to play targeted melodies, he or she might notice that all the notes needed to accomplish some melodies don't seem to exist on the instrument. That is because the 10-hole diatonic harmonica has only seven of the 12 notes that make up the chromatic scale. On a C harmonica, the available notes are A, B, C, D, E, F, and G. These notes are repeated at least once in the course of the three-octave range of the instrument.

The chromatic scale is a series of 12 notes that the Western system of musical notation employs to comprise a complete scale. So, unlike the guitar, violin, or piano, some notes are indeed missing. On a C harmonica, the missing notes are A♭, B♭, D♭, E♭, and G♭.

The diatonic harmonica was not originally designed to play the chromatic scale. It was a lucky accident that, at some point in the history of the instrument—perhaps around the late 1800s—someone realized that by changing your embouchure (the configuration of the tongue, lips, and the other muscles in your mouth) it was possible to change the pitches of some of the notes on the harmonica by using a technique now known as note "bending." This resulted in a larger selection of the chromatic notes being available.

Although this is taken for granted these days, it must have been quite a revelation when note bending was first discovered. It was an important enough innovation that note bending has become a standard skill for most modern 10-hole diatonic harmonica players. Without this skill, obvious melodic limitations are placed on the instrument. Even with note bending, some notes of the chromatic scale are still not available on the harmonica, so access to the chromatic scale is expanded with the addition of note bending, but not completed.

This book's primary focus is an organized approach to bending notes and incorporating them into blues playing. The book offers information on all the bent notes on the diatonic harmonica individually. There are eight low-register and mid-range bent notes, and four high-register note bends, all of which move the notes down a half step. On some holes, there is more than one bend, which I refer to as incremental bends. Since there are no frets or other definite delineations between bent and un-bent notes, it is possible to bend some notes just a little short of, or a little past, a half step. More on that later.

In addition to offering an organized approach to bending, I will also offer some information on overblowing—a technique that allows for playing the notes that are still missing from the complete chromatic scale—after mastering all of the more common bends.

The range of the 10-hole harmonica is three octaves, and I will be referring to the octaves as the low register, the middle register, and the high register. Low notes and high notes are bent in different ways. Low- and middle-register notes are bent while playing inhale notes. High-register notes are bent while playing exhale notes. The bends all involve changes in embouchure, and each bend has an incrementally different embouchure.

This book is intended to help the intermediate harmonica player improve and move to the next level. Learning to master all the bent notes and starting to incorporate overblowing allows for the opportunity to play the harmonica with a more chromatic approach.

This book will be more helpful to a harmonica player with some ability to bend notes, but it does include instruction to help the beginner learn to isolate single notes and to begin bending. Also included are ways to incorporate these bent notes into blues playing, both in short musical phrases and also over the most basic 12-bar blues progression, which will also be explained.

One traditional approach to playing blues harmonica is to learn "licks" or "riffs," that is, short musical phrases that often are repeated. This is a traditional approach and an excellent way to learn how to play blues harmonica. Many licks involve some amount of note bending. By mastering all the bent notes and incorporating them into your playing, you will be able to play all that has come before by innovators like Little Walter, Sonny Terry, Sonny Boy Williamson, and others—or they might be of your own creation. Many of the examples presented here function well as "blues licks" and can be used as a starting point for becoming a consummate blues harp player. For those interested in a compendium of traditional blues licks, I recommend checking out *100 Authentic Blues Harmonica Licks*, another of my offerings from Hal Leonard.

It will take some students longer than others to learn how to bend notes. Leaning to bend involves trial and error. Some frustration may occur, but eventually, with persistence, a bent note will pop in for you; with practice, you will be able to bend it again with less difficulty. Gradually, you will be able to play it consistently, and eventually you will be able to incorporate it into a musical phrase and sound natural doing it. And then, on to the next bent note. Make sure you spend time practicing, as without practice, there will be no progress.

Tongue Blocking vs. The Pucker Method

As mentioned earlier, everything happens inside the instrument and inside your mouth, so you'll never be able to actually see how to position your mouth to form the embouchure needed to bend a note. Here are some instructions, though, that will help you achieve it; when it happens, you will feel it and you will hear it.

The first step is to get a clear, solid single note. There are two main methods for getting single notes: **tongue blocking** and the **pucker method**. There are differences in how notes are produced by these two methods, and also some tonal differences.

In tongue blocking, the right side of your mouth forms a wall where air cannot pass through the next higher hole than the hole you want to play, and your tongue blocks the hole that is one note lower than the note you want to play. You are essentially boxing out a note with your tongue on one side and the right side of your mouth on the other.

The pucker method is just as it is named: you pucker your lips around the hole you want to play. The embouchure is similar to drinking through a little cocktail straw. With practice, you can learn exactly the size of this narrow area, and with muscle memory, you should be able to move around on the harmonica and get clean and solid single notes with only a little practice.

I find that tongue blocking makes it more difficult to bend notes accurately; it also makes it harder to play fast, articulate lines. There are times when the tone produced by tongue blocking is appropriate to blues playing. Other times, the tone produced by the pucker method will be more appropriate. Blues harp players often gravitate to an amplified sound. Usually, some sound distortion of a desirable kind is involved, which obscures many of the natural nuances of playing unamplified and negates some of the tonal difference between tongue blocking and the pucker method. In a typical performance, I alternate between acoustic and amplified sounds, as well as between tongue blocking and the pucker method. With experience, you will find that the individual song and the style of accompaniment dictate what approach to use.

Note that when trying to bend notes using either method, you must have a solid seal where your lips meet the harmonica. All the air needs to go through the reed you are bending: the seal must be solid enough that no air leaks where your mouth meets the harmonica, but not so rigid as to prevent you from sliding the harmonica through your lips to move from one hole to another without pulling the instrument away from your lips.

If your interest is in performing music that involves playing alternate multiple voicings—that is, bounces back and forth between bass notes and higher-register melodies—tongue blocking is essential. If you want to play genres that are mostly dependent on single-note lines, the pucker method will serve you well. The exception to this generality is that masterful blues playing involves the use of certain chords and octaves, and tongue blocking is the only way to achieve some of these effects. So even if you are committing to the pucker method for note bending, keep an open mind and learn how to tongue block as well. As mentioned earlier, I use a combination of pucker method and tongue blocking in my playing.

How to Isolate Single Notes

If you can't isolate single notes, you will be unable to bend notes. As a first step then, isolating single notes is crucial. Here is a simple exercise that can help you get the feel of playing single notes without a lot of technique. Although you're just sliding from one adjacent note to the next, make an effort to give each note the same time value. Be sure that all the air is going through the reeds and none is escaping where the harp meets your lips. Again, I recommend the pucker method. Take a listen to this example:

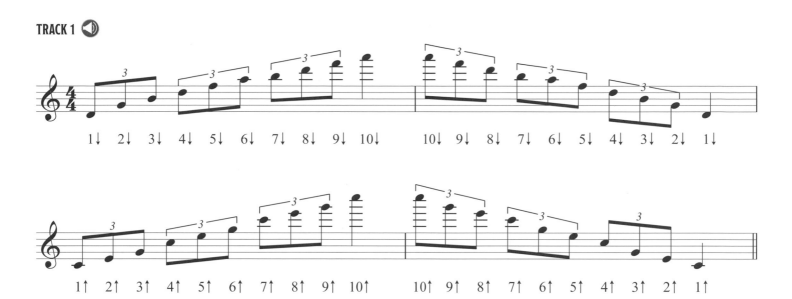

Once you feel comfortable doing this, slow it down and play the notes with a consciousness about maintaining the integrity of strong, clear notes, as well as uniform duration:

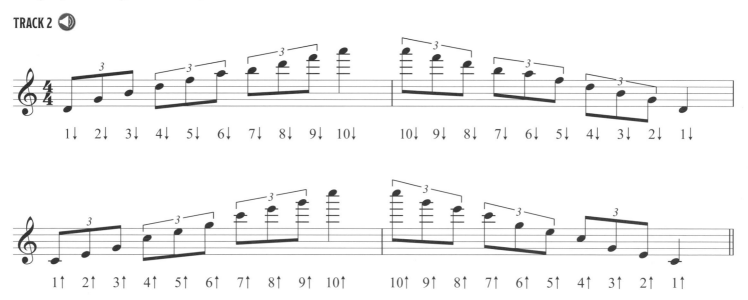

Playing Blues on the Harmonica—The Idea of Cross Harp and Different Positions

New musical opportunities became available when it was discovered that the harmonica could be played in a different key than the one in which it is pitched. In most blues harmonica playing, this has boiled down to playing the harmonica in three different keys:

> **1st position** refers to playing a harp pitched in the same key as the song: use your C harp for songs in the key of C.
>
> **2nd position** refers to playing a harmonica that is four scale degrees up from the key of the song: use your C harp for songs in the key of G.
>
> **3rd position** refers to playing a harmonica that's one whole step down from the key of the song: use your C harp for songs in the key of D.

Early on, I mentioned that it's easy to get a pleasant musical sound out of the harmonica just by breathing in and out through the reeds. Campfire songs and folk music like "Home on the Range," "Oh! Susanna," and "You Are My Sunshine" are songs that are easy to play in 1st position. This book, however, is specifically about playing blues. Although some blues playing is done in 1st position (most notably, high note soloing, which we will explore), most blues harmonica playing is done by playing your harmonica in 2nd position. Playing in 2nd position is one way in which we are more readily able to access more of the "blue notes" because the draw notes in the low register are where we find the most bent notes. To some extent, use of the blues notes (flatted-3rds, -5ths, and -7ths) is an important element that helps define blues playing. Be aware, as we start talking about bending notes, that many of the bends on the low end of the harp are played in 2nd position. Later in the book when we explore high-note bends, much of the playing will be in 1st position; that is, playing your C harp in the key of C. At the end of the book, there are examples of blues playing in all three positions.

Note that, in 2nd position, the draw notes most readily correspond to the I chord and the blow notes most readily correspond to the IV chord. A brief explanation of the 12-bar form will help explain why this is significant.

The 12-Bar Blues Form

A large percentage of blues songs have a fairly strict relationship of underlying chords. That relationship is often in a 12-bar form or a variation of the 12-bar form. A bar consists of four uniformly timed beats. In the basic 12-bar form, there are usually three chords involved. They are the I chord, which is the key of the song, the IV chord, four scale degrees up from the key of the song, and the V chord, five scale degrees above the key of the song. In the key of G these chords are G, C, and D, respectively. Note that in 2nd position, your C harmonica is pitched four scale degrees above the key of the song: G, the I chord.

The basic 12-bar blues structure is this:

I I I I IV IV I I V IV I I

Or in the key of G:

G G G G C C G G D C G G
1 2 3 4 5 6 7 8 9 10 11 12

Of these 12 bars, eight are over the I chord (two-thirds of the entire progression). In 2nd position, the inhale notes most readily play over the I chord; these are, not coincidentally, the notes that contain the eight low- and middle-register bent notes, so playing over the I chord offers the most melodic possibilities, and also contains the bulk of the progression.

On the low end of your C harmonica, the G note (key of the song) or I chord root note, is 2-draw or 3-blow—they are the same note. The root of the IV chord, C, is 1-blow. The D note, or root of the V chord, is 1-draw. You can play over the blues chord progression most easily by simply playing the root note of the chords over the changes, like this:

TRACK 3 🔊   TRACK 3 PLAY ALONG 🔊

Licks cannot be perfectly transposed until we can bend notes, so these IV and V chord transpositions are adjusted approximations. Here's a simple blues boogie-woogie-based riff loosely transposed to move over the three chords and fit the structure of a basic 12-bar blues:

TRACK 4  TRACK 4 PLAY ALONG

At the end of the section on bending low notes, track 35 demonstrates the full boogie woogie riff with the complete line transposed over all three chords of the 12-bar, and played over the basic 12-bar form. The complete version involves several bends. The basic boogie woogie 12-bar riff is also played in track 102, using overblows in the middle register and high-note bends in the upper register.

In general, if any of the exercises in this book give you trouble, play them slowly until you can play them cleanly, then pick up the speed to match the original tempo of the audio track.

As mentioned earlier, the 2-draw plays the same note as the 3-blow (the low G note on a C harmonica); depending on the context of the musical phrase you are playing, one or the other may be used to play that note, according to your preference.

Bending the Low Notes–How to Do It

Because of differences in human physiology and the differences in individual harmonica construction, certain notes will be easier to bend than others for different people. So, if a particular hole is not responding to your efforts to bend, try a different hole. For most people, once a bend falls into place, the others will follow.

Because you can't see the inside of your mouth to try and match up how to move the muscles to achieve the embouchure to produce a bent note, we can only attempt to describe it.

Please note that drawing really hard and loud will not help notes bend! It's entirely about finding the correct embouchure.

Bending Basics

As mentioned earlier, two basics you must master before bending will occur are:

1. A good seal where the harp meets your mouth, so that all the air is going through the reed, and none is escaping where the harp meets your lips.

2. A solid *single* note, not a combination of two or more notes—at least to begin.

There are three strategies you should try to employ simultaneously when learning to bend. Try them individually, then try to do them simultaneously.

Start by playing a solid single note on the 1 hole, the lowest hole. First exhale to empty the air in your lungs, then form a seal over the 1 hole to get a solid single note and inhale to play a note so that all the air is going through the reed and no air is leaking where the harmonica meets your mouth.

1. **Jaw position**: While inhaling a single note to bend, try lowering your jaw slightly, and also moving it forward a little bit, mimicking how a caveman might talk.

2. **Tongue position**: As you lower your jaw, make your tongue concave and lower it against the floor of your mouth. Also, try to curl the tip of your tongue behind your front bottom teeth.

3. **Vowel shape of your mouth**: Perhaps most importantly, after playing the natural note, try changing the vowel shape of your lips and mouth from "dwee" to "oh." While drawing air in and mouthing "dwee-oh," the "dwee" should be the natural note, the "oh" the bent note. You should be constricting the muscles in your mouth to make your mouth a narrower chamber through which air is passing.

It seems like a lot of things to be thinking about at once, but if you try it enough times, eventually you won't have to think about maintaining an airtight seal, or that you are isolating a single note. Instead, you can focus more on changing your embouchure in such a way that makes the note change pitch.

Whether or not you are able to bend the 1-draw, experiment with the same process on a different hole. The 1-draw is a good starting point because there are no holes below the 1 hole. You're getting help with the pucker method by virtue of it being the lowest hole. However, the longer, lower reeds can be harder to bend when you are starting out.

Next, try inhaling a strong single note on the 4 hole. This might be a little harder than the 1 hole because you do not have a natural end below the 4 hole, and you must employ a good pucker to isolate the note from both sides. However, because of our physical differences, the 4 hole might be easier to bend than the 1 hole was. Also, a shorter, higher-pitched reed might be more easily bent. Also try the 2 hole and the 3 hole.

If you are able to bend the 2 or 3 hole, understand that there are multiple, incremental bends on those two holes. Refinement will eventually be necessary, but more on that later. Note that all these bends— when achieved properly— will result in the natural note going lower by, ideally, a half step. For example, the unbent 1-draw on a C harp is a D note. If you bend it properly, it will go all the way down to a D♭ note. The 4 hole is also a D note, just one octave higher. If you have access to a piano or a guitar, you can match up the notes to make sure you are bending it all the way down a half step, or play into an electronic tuning device to check. Of course, all the audio tracks accompanying this book are being played in tune.

To review, in addition to having a tight seal and not playing more than one note at a time, here are the three essential building blocks of note bending: 1.) While you inhale, experiment with moving your jaw forward and lowering it slightly. 2.) While changing the position of your jaw, try to further change the vowel shape of your mouth by pretending to say— while inhaling—the word "dwee-oh" (the "dwee" is the natural note, the "oh" is the bent note). 3.) Make your tongue flat against the floor of your mouth and curl the tip up behind your bottom front teeth. These techniques should be employed while making sure that all the air is going through the reed and no air is escaping where the harp meets your mouth. If all the air is not making it through the reed, the reed will not bend.

Playing Bends in Tune—Muscle Memory, Playing by Ear, and Building Stamina

This is a good place to introduce the concept of "tuning while you play." Since playing a bent note is not automatically an absolutely in-tune note like one produced by a piano key or guitar fret, it is possible to partially bend a note and not actually be playing it in tune. Make a mental note that, as you are bending a note, you are also tuning it. When bending notes, you are actually playing through the microtones that occur in between notes, much like sliding between notes on a fretless instrument like the violin, or using a pitch bender on an electronic keyboard.

There is another related point here. With this book, you are learning to play by ear. With practice, you are training your ear to hear when the notes are being played in tune and when they are not. You are also training your mouth to remember how to fall into the correct embouchure for each of the bends, and there is an incremental difference in embouchure for each of the bends. This is where muscle memory comes into play.

You are training yourself to have an instinct about which embouchure to form when you want to play a particular bent note, and part of that involves forming the embouchure that will produce an *in tune* bent note. Don't fixate on this right now, but be mindful of it going forward. Eventually, with practice, this will come naturally, with no thought needed.

There is something to be said about the organic quality of playing notes that aren't 100 percent perfectly in tune. It adds a human, voice-like element to playing the harmonica. This is a good feature that many other instruments do not have.

Also important, and related to muscle memory, is the concept of stamina. Even as you are developing muscle memory, you are strengthening the muscles needed to achieve these particular bent notes. Some of the muscles in your mouth used for bending notes are muscles you have not used with this kind of focus before. Your practice will naturally lead you to strengthen the muscles you need to hit bent notes, and hit them accurately. Holding the bent note as long as you can is one good way to help these muscles to develop, and to promote muscle memory. Just be sure to maintain the integrity of the tuning while doing this.

Please note that the following low- and high-note bending exercises and examples will all be played on a C harmonica.

While you will eventually be incorporating bent notes into your playing, at the beginning your focus should simply be to achieve the bends.

There are eight low- and mid-range bent notes plus one implied bend, and four high-register note bends plus three implied bends. On the 2, 3, and 10 holes, there are multiple bends, which I refer to as incremental bends.

BENDS ON THE LOW NOTES

Next, you'll probably want to figure out which is the easiest note for you to bend. For most people, it's either the 1-hole bend or the 4-hole bend. I'm going to start with the bend on the 1 hole and work my way up the low end of the harmonica, just to have a logical protocol. If you are having trouble bending the 1 hole after trying it for a while, jump ahead to the 4-hole bend, then return to the 1 hole once you have the 4-hole bend down. Or try to bend on the 2 or 3 hole. Eventually, you'll want to learn all the bends.

One more important detail: bending on the 1 and 2 holes involves creating a larger space inside your mouth. Bending on the 3 through 6 holes involves making the space in your mouth smaller. So, when bending holes 1 and 2, you should be lowering your jaw, and when bending holes 3 through 6, you should be raising your jaw. It's a little different for everyone, so experiment until you find an embouchure that works.

The 1-Hole Draw Bend

At its most basic, here's how the 1-hole bend sounds and looks in notation:

TRACK 5 🔊

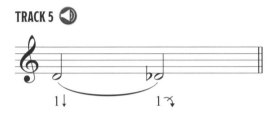

If you're just starting to bend, a good way to start reinforcing your ability to bend consistently—once you can achieve this first bend—is to go back and forth between the natural note and the bent note, over and over. If you aren't bending all the way down, in tune, stop and let your mouth rest, then try again. This goes for all the bent notes that follow.

Till now, we've been focusing on bending notes a half step flat. In the text, as well as in the previous music example, the bent note has been written as D-flat (D♭). Another name for D-flat is C-sharp (C♯). Since we're bending back and forth several times in this next example, it's easier to read if the bent note is written as C-sharp.

An important rule in music notation states that when you have a sharp or a flat on a particular note in a measure—in this case, the sharp is on C—the sharp affects all Cs that follow in that measure, making them all C♯s. That's why the harmonica tab for the second note is the same as the tab for the fourth note (by the way, the vertical lines on the five-line note staff indicate the measure breaks and are called bar lines.) Remember the 12-bar blues we talked about a bit earlier?

I'd like to point out one more thing: notice the curved line that runs from the first to the last note. This symbol is called a **slur**. A slur is used to connect a series of notes that are smoothly bent and released. Enough talk—let's play it!

TRACK 6 🔊

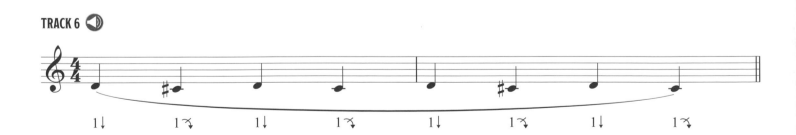

The following exercises will help you start to get comfortable with bending the 1 hole. Note that there is a difference in difficulty between starting with the natural (un-bent) 1 hole and bending down, as in the first two notes, versus starting with the bent note "cold" and releasing the bend to play the natural note again, as in the fourth and fifth notes. This exercise forces you to play it both ways, and there will be a similar exercise for all the following holes. Including the blow note here, this musical phrase is a chromatic run; that is, you will be playing what would be three notes right next to each other on a keyboard or guitar neck:

TRACK 7

Here's a lick based on a bebop melody that employs the 1-hole bend:

TRACK 8

This little musical phrase uses only the 1-hole bend:

TRACK 9

Sometimes, a lick might start on the bent note on the 1 hole:

TRACK 10

The 2-Hole Draw Bends

There are some differences between bending on the 2 hole and bending on the 1 hole. As I mentioned earlier, each bend has a different embouchure. So, as you have already done with the 1 hole, you'll need to experiment with your embouchure. The vowel shape of your mouth, and the incremental movement of your lower jaw while maintaining a good seal where the harp meets your lips, is what's needed to get the 2 hole to bend down. Reminder: all the air must be going through only the 2 hole—no chords!

There are two different bent notes available on the second hole, which multiplies the difficulty factor of the 2-hole bends. The first bend lowers the pitch by a half step, and the second bend lowers the pitch an additional half step. So, there are actually three notes available on the 2-hole draw: G, Gb, and F. I call these incremental bends. You'll need to shift your embouchure ever so slightly to articulate both bent notes. Here's how it looks, starting with the natural un-bent note:

TRACK 11 🔊

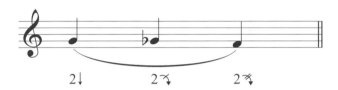

In the harmonica tab, notice the curved bend arrow below the last note has two hatch marks. This indicates a bend of two half steps (AKA a whole step).

You will want to locate all three notes and try to lock in on playing them in tune. As on the 1 hole, this exercise forces you to start with the natural note. Work your way through the half- and whole-step bends, then play the blow note. The next, more difficult step is to hit the second, lower bend "cold," then the first bend, and finally to release the bend in order to get back to the natural 2-hole note. This is a four-note chromatic sequence.

The half-step bend in the first measure is written as a Gb, while it's written as an F# in the second measure—two names for the same note. Also notice that there isn't a slur connecting the notes. I'm playing each note with a bit of separation this time:

TRACK 12 🔊

In this example, there's a bit more separation between the bent notes. This is indicated by the small dots below these notes, which are called **staccato** marks. Take a look at these two versions of a bluesy lick, incorporating all three notes available on the 2-hole draw:

TRACK 13 🔊

The term "bounce back" refers to alternating between two adjacent holes. Here's an example:

TRACK 15 🔊

If you're really getting the hang of things, this harder variation involves a deep bend and a bounce back:

TRACK 16 🔊

This bounce back lick moves from a whole step bend to a half step bend to a 2 draw:

TRACK 17 🔊

The 3-Hole Draw Bends

The 3-hole draw has three distinct bends plus the natural note. It's the only hole that has a total of four possible notes. Because of the number of incremental bends, it is perhaps the most difficult group of bends to master.

Here's how the four notes that you get from the 3 hole sound:

TRACK 18 🔊

The chromatic bending exercise on the 3 hole looks like this:

TRACK 19

Another way to approach this exercise involves jumping from the natural note to each of the three bends separately, with a bounce back to the tonic:

TRACK 20

This bluesy lick alternates the 2 hole with the 3-hole bends:

TRACK 21

The 4-Hole Draw Bend

By the time you get to the 4-hole bend, you are back to only one available bend. The natural note and the bent note are the same notes as the 1-hole draw, just one octave higher. Here's how it sounds:

TRACK 22

Here's how it looks as a chromatic exercise:

TRACK 23

As mentioned earlier, for some people, this may be the easiest bend to achieve as a first bend on a C harmonica.

The triplet in this exercise makes you work the 4-hole bend but starts on the natural note. These are eighth-note triplets—three evenly spaced notes per beat:

TRACK 24

4↓   4↘   3↓   4↓   4↘   3↓   4↓   4↘   3↓   2↓

Now try a triplet that starts on the 4-hole bend:

TRACK 25

4↘   4↓   5↓   4↘   4↓   5↓   4↘   4↓   5↓   4↘ 4↓

If you blend the previous two licks together, it might sound something like this:

TRACK 26

4↘ 4↓ 5↓ 4↓ 4↘ 3↓   4↘ 4↓ 5↓ 4↓ 4↘ 3↓   4↘ 4↓ 5↓ 4↓ 4↘ 3↓ 4↘ 4↓

A **glissando** is a quick ascending or descending series of all-drawn or all-blown notes on consecutive holes. The glissando in this example leads to a pair of 4-hole bends:

TRACK 27

1↓ 2↓ 3↓ 4↓   4↘ 4↓   4↘ 4↓   3↓   1↓ 2↓ 3↓ 4↓   4↘ 4↓   4↘ 4↓   2↓

You might recognize this tune that utilizes the 4-hole draw:

TRACK 28

4↓   4↘   4↓   4↑   4↓   4↘   4↓   4↑   4↓   4↘   4↓

3↓   4↓   4↘   4↓   3↓   4↓   4↘   4↓   5↑   4↓   4↘   4↓

5↑   4↓   4↘   4↓   6↑   4↓   4↘   4↓   6↑

The 5-Hole Implied Bend

There is a bend on the 5 hole, but it does not bend an entire half step. I think of it as an implied bend. It's useful for coloring a note or phrase, but to go down an entire half step, you'll need to play the 5-hole blow.

This is a good place to talk about the implications of playing out of tune with intention. I find that, on occasion, it creates constructive tension to play a bend that is not quite in tune. Note that there is a difference between playing out of tune because of imprecise playing, and playing out of tune with purpose. Playing a bend out of tune can sound good in context, but it's not likely to sound right unless it's done with a plan.

So back to the 5-hole draw. You'll only be able to bend it down a quarter step, hence there's no slash on the bend arrow. Here's how it sounds by itself:

TRACK 29 🔊

And here's how it sounds in our standard bending exercise:

TRACK 30 🔊

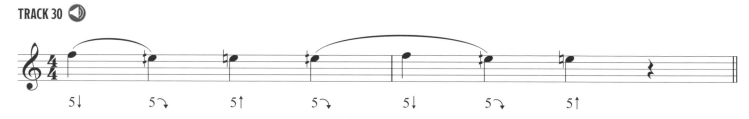

In this exercise, the first and third triplets use the bent note, while the second and fourth triplets use the blow note. You can hear the subtle difference between the pitch of the 5-hole bend and the 5-hole blow:

TRACK 31 🔊

The 6-Hole Draw Bend

There's one bend on the 6-hole draw. Here's how the 6-hole draw sounds:

TRACK 32 🔊

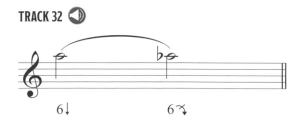

And here's how the 6 hole sounds as a chromatic exercise:

TRACK 33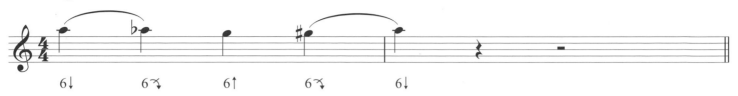

6↓   6↘   6↑   6↘   6↓

Bending the 6-hole works well in 2nd position over the V chord of a 12-bar blues progression, or over the I chord in 3rd position:

TRACK 34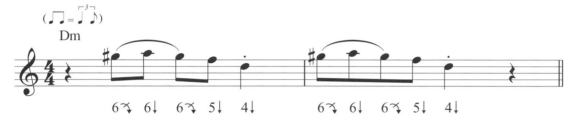

6↘ 6↓ 6↘ 5↓ 4↓   6↘ 6↓ 6↘ 5↓ 4↓

This completes the available bent notes in the low and middle registers. Below is a more developed version of the boogie woogie riff, utilizing bent notes and played over a basic 12-bar blues progression:

TRACK 35

2↓ 3↓ 4↓ 5↑   5↓ 5↑ 4↓ 3↓   2↓ 3↓ 4↓ 5↑   5↓ 5↑ 4↓ 3↓

1↑ 2↑ 3↑ 3↘   3↘ 3↘ 2↓ 2↑   2↓ 3↓ 4↓ 5↑   5↓ 5↑ 4↓ 3↓

1↓ 2↘ 3↘ 3↓   1↑ 2↑ 3↑ 3↘   2↓ 3↓ 4↓ 5↑   5↓ 5↑ 4↓ 3↓ 2↓

COMBINING OTHER TECHNIQUES WITH BENDS TO COLOR NOTES

In addition to mastering the bent notes, "coloring" the notes to add interest for the listener and for yourself is another way to take your playing to the next level. Up until this point, we've been working on strategies to simply play the bent notes and incorporate them into easy licks, but you can add color to the notes to give them more life and make them sound a little different than each other in a few different ways. It's possible to play a musical phrase in a manner that correctly executes the notes, but conveys little feeling and sounds more like an exercise than living music. Here are several techniques you can use to add life and color to notes and phrases. The list of effects below can be applied to bent notes as well as natural notes.

1. **Double stops**: two notes played simultaneously to add dimension beyond single notes

2. **"Warble:"** trill effect (going rapidly back and forth between two adjacent holes)

3. **Vibrato:** pulsating effect achieved using various techniques

4. **Dynamics**: variation of the volume and attack

Bending While Playing Pairs of Notes

Once you have a good handle on bending single notes, you can challenge yourself with some more advanced bending. To play two notes simultaneously (called a double stop), widen your pucker to play two adjacent holes at once. It's possible to bend a note while playing a double stop on the low end of the harp, all the way from the 1-2 combination to the 4-5 combination. You may notice that all these two-hole combinations involve bending the lower of the two notes, not both at once. Here are some examples:

TRACK 36

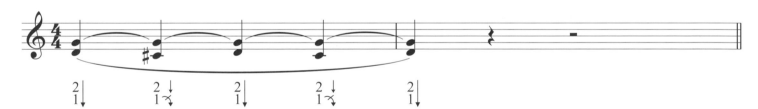

TRACK 37

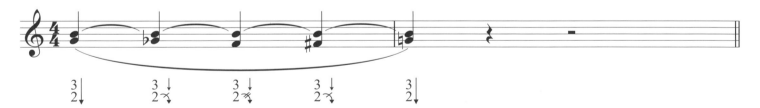

TRACK 38

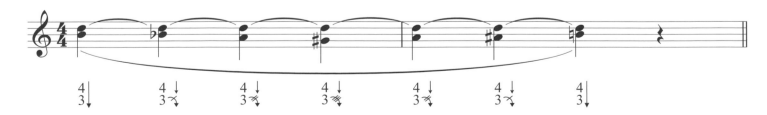

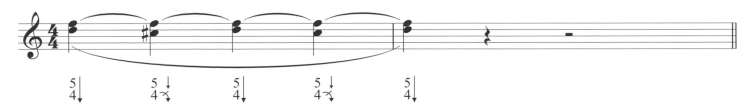

The lick below includes repeat signs (𝄆 𝄇) around the first two measures, so play the first line of music twice. This bluesy lick employs double-stop bends played over a 12-bar progression:

TRACK 40 🔊   **TRACK 40 PLAY ALONG** 🔊

There are many classic licks that use bent double stops, like this one:

TRACK 41

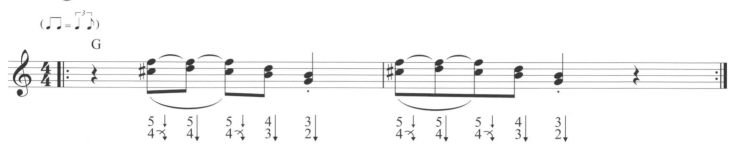

When transitioning from the I to the IV chord in the fourth bar of a blues progression, this lick can come in handy. The first example is in single notes, the second example uses bent double stops:

TRACK 42

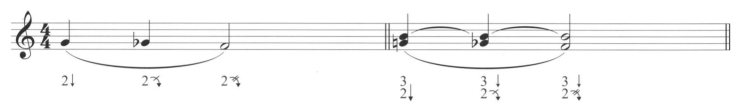

Any place you can bend a note, you may find it appropriate to bend it as a double stop instead. Try these bent double stops played over a 12-bar progression:

TRACK 43   TRACK 43 PLAY ALONG

Bending While Playing Warbles

Just as in bending double stops, if you take two adjacent holes and play them alternately in rapid succession, you get a trill. This is sometimes referred to as a "warble" or "shake." It is possible to bend while using the warble technique. Generally, only the lower of the two notes is bent for this effect.

Here's how a simple warble bend looks using four different combinations:

TRACK 44

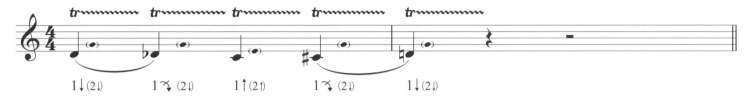

TRACK 45

TRACK 46

TRACK 47

The speed with which you alternate between the two notes creates another level of interest:

TRACK 48

Slow warble
Medium warble
Fast warble

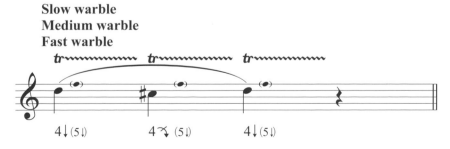

Most trills are best controlled by holding the harp stationary and waggling your head incrementally to achieve the slow and medium warbles in the previous demonstration. However, for the third and fastest warble in the previous example, I am using my hands to move the harmonica while holding my head stationary. For every trill, it is important to have a solid foundation or stance for the way you are holding the harmonica to gain control over the speed with which you are alternating between notes when executing a warble.

Take a look at this bluesy warble riff played over a 12-bar progression:

Adding Vibrato to Bent Notes and Double Stops

There are a few different harmonica vibratos. These can be applied not only to single notes, but also to bent double stops and bent-note warbles.

Throat Vibrato

Many blues players like to use a throat or diaphragm vibrato when playing single notes, chords, and bent notes. Each of these examples first plays a single note with a bend, then a double stop with a bend—both with throat vibrato:

TRACK 50

*Throat vibrato throughout

TRACK 51

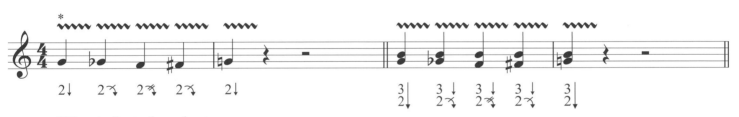

*Throat vibrato throughout

TRACK 52

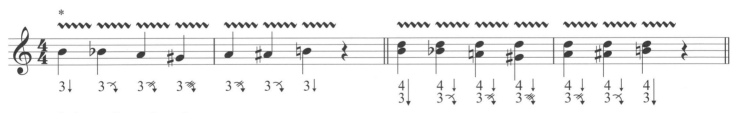

*Throat vibrato throughout

Jaw Vibrato

Although it is possible to play any of these combinations with throat vibrato, there will be times when you may find it's easier to control the vibrato pulses with "jaw vibrato." It's good to develop this as an option for playing single notes (bent or natural), then using it to add vibrato when playing double stops and bent double stops.

While playing the selected note, evenly lower and raise your jaw incrementally to create the vibrato effect. The farther you lower your jaw, the more pronounced the vibrato will be. Your tongue should be down on the floor of your mouth. Here's how it's done:

TRACK 53

TRACK 54

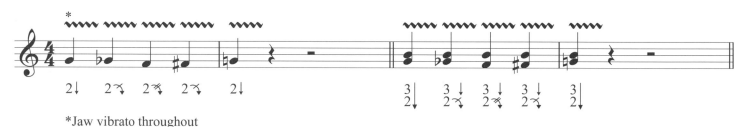

TRACK 55

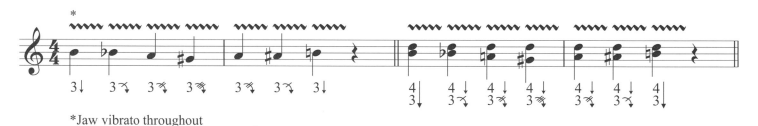

The Ruffle Vibrato

This is another type of vibrato, achieved by moving your uvula and soft palate. It has a distinctive, rough sound, probably not appropriate for all occasions, but applicable as a special effect. Take a listen:

TRACK 56

Hand-Wah Vibrato

Hand wah is another kind of vibrato. This does not require any adjustment to your embouchure. I use my left hand to hold the harp stationary while pivoting my cupped right hand for this technique. The tighter the seal between the back edges of your hands below the bottom joint of your little finger, the more pronounced this effect will be. Like the warble, the speed with which you fan your hand affects the sound. This is how it sounds:

TRACK 57

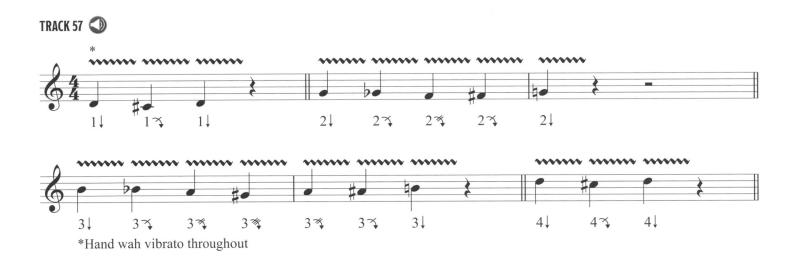

*Hand wah vibrato throughout

Dynamics

You can add life to musical phrases by changing the volume and intensity of the attack. When you are talking, you don't say every word with the same volume or intensity. Our language provides the opportunity for expression and to alter meaning by changing inflection, volume, and emphasis on certain syllables and words. Without this, we would talk in a monotone like robots. The same is true of the language of music. If you don't change volume (dynamics) or emphasis (attack), the music might sound lifeless. This is true for natural notes as well as bent notes. Hitting bent notes in tune is not dependent on playing hard. To have full control of the bent notes, it's important to be able to hit the bends "cold" at a low volume.

BENDS ON THE HIGH NOTES

Some Considerations Regarding High-Note Bends

Just as the low-note bends each go down a half step per bend, so do the high-note bends. One difference is that low-note bends are achieved on draw notes, while high-note bends are executed on blow notes. Each embouchure for this set of bends is slightly different, just as it is for the low-note bends.

It's going to be difficult to gain control of the high-note bends, especially on hole 10, if you are not using a decent quality C harmonica. And even on a good one, response will vary widely from harp to harp. For example, in the course of writing this book, I have had five different C harmonicas lined up on my desk. One works better than the others for high-note bends. Another one works better for overblows. A different one plays more easily when articulating the bent notes while playing double stops, etc. Response will be different from harp to harp. The same holds true for low-note bends. Certain harps hit the bends easier and cleaner. You will also find that different keyed harps respond to bending more readily than others. It's worth experimenting with these bending exercises on different keyed harps if you have them. In general, *higher* pitched harps bend the *low* notes more easily, and *lower* pitched harps bend the *high* notes more easily when starting out. With more experience, this matters less.

If you are new to high-note bending and things are not going well on your C harp, start on a lower pitched-harmonica, like a low G, Ab, A, Bb, or B. The C harmonica is the highest-pitched harmonica for relatively easy high-note bending. You can still utilize the tablature, although the recorded examples will be in a different key. Control of bent high notes will become easier on your C harp as you move down from the 10 hole to the 9 hole to the 8 hole.

For the individual high-note bends, I'm going to start on the 10 hole and work my way down just for the sake of having a logical protocol. There are two bends on 10, one bend and an implied bend on 9, one bend and an implied bend on 8, and one implied bend on 7. Some of these bends are a little harder to incorporate into regular blues soloing, but there's a time and a place for all of them, so you should try to learn them all.

High-Note Bending Embouchure

There is a different configuration of your mouth muscles for high-note bending than for low-note bending. With high-note bends, you move your jaw forward, purse your lips outward, and constrict the inner area of your mouth cavity. As in low-note bending, you might consider changing the vowel shape of your mouth using the syllables "dee-oh," where the "dee" is the natural note and the "oh" is the bent note. Tongue position is also important. To bend, you need to push your tongue forward in your mouth and curve the middle upward toward the roof of your mouth. As in low-note bends, a certain amount of experimentation is required. If you struggle long enough, eventually a high-note bend will pop in for you. If the 10 hole isn't bending, try the 9 hole, then the 8 hole. It is likely that the 8-hole bend will be easier at first than the 9- and 10-hole bends on your C harmonica.

The next few sets of exercises and licks use high-note bends. There is more chromatic flexibility over blues changes in 1st position with high-note bending, so these licks will be played on a C harp in the key of C.

10-Hole Blow Bends

Here's how the high-note bends on hole 10 sound:

TRACK 58 🔊

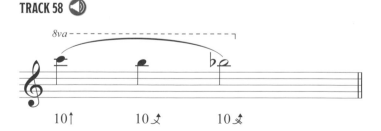

Let's look at the 10-hole bends in our exercise format, as a chromatic run:

TRACK 59 🔊

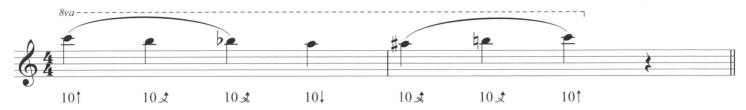

Another good exercise employing the 10-hole bends involves a bounce back to the 9-blow:

TRACK 60 🔊

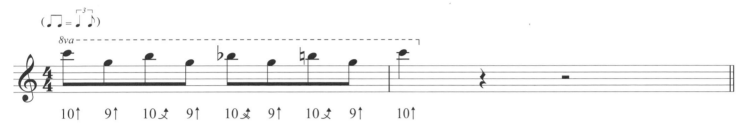

This bluesy lick employs the 10-hole bends, and can be used over the I chord in the key of C:

TRACK 61 🔊

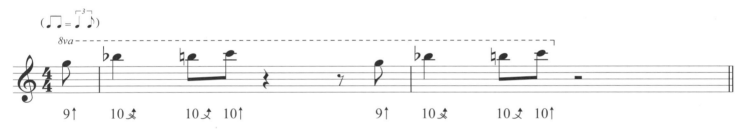

9-Hole Blow Bends

When bending the 9 hole, it is possible to bend slightly lower than the target G♭ note. This lower bend is an implied bend, since it won't bend all the way down to F; use your ear to make sure you're not bending too far. Here's how the 9-hole bend sounds:

TRACK 62 🔊

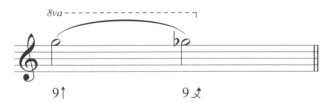

The second, implied bend on the 9-hole bend sounds like this in our standard chromatic scale exercise:

TRACK 63 🔊

Try this nice little lick that employs the 9-blow bend:

TRACK 64

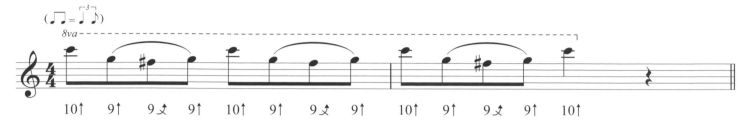

10↑ 9↑ 9↗ 9↑ 10↑ 9↑ 9↗ 9↑ 10↑ 9↑ 9↗ 9↑ 10↑

Bending from the natural 10 hole to the second bend (a whole step below the natural note) is a well-known, versatile lick, often played over the IV chord (C) of a G blues progression:

TRACK 65

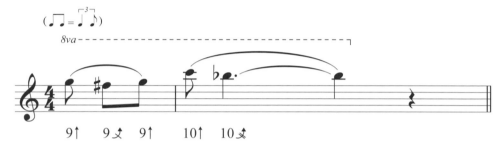

9↑ 9↗ 9↑ 10↑ 10↗

9-hole bends in 1st position are perfect for this classic turnaround lick, which also includes a bounce back to the 10-hole blow:

TRACK 66

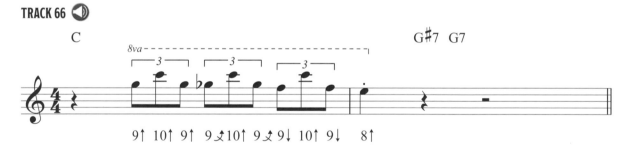

9↑ 10↑ 9↑ 9↗10↑ 9↗ 9↓ 10↑ 9↓ 8↑

Bouncing between the 8-hole and the 9-hole notes with a bend on the 9 sounds like this:

TRACK 67

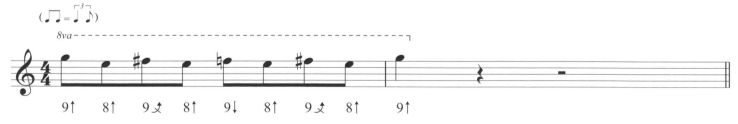

9↑ 8↑ 9↗ 8↑ 9↓ 8↑ 9↗ 8↑ 9↑

Now let's try some triplets using the 9-hole bends:

TRACK 68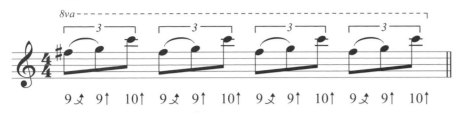

9↗ 9↑ 10↑ 9↗ 9↑ 10↑ 9↗ 9↑ 10↑ 9↗ 9↑ 10↑

TRACK 69

9↑ 9↗ 8↑ 9↑ 9↗ 8↑ 9↑ 9↗ 8↑ 9↑ 9↗ 8↑

Put these two triplets together and it looks like this:

TRACK 70

9↗ 9↑ 10↑ 9↑ 9↗ 8↑ 9↗ 9↑ 10↑ 9↑ 9↗ 8↑ 9↗ 9↑ 10↑ 9↑ 9↗ 8↑ 9↗ 9↑

This familiar melody plays pretty easily using the 9-hole bends. It's the same melody we played on track 28 in 2nd position in the key of G. Here's how it is played in the key of C:

TRACK 71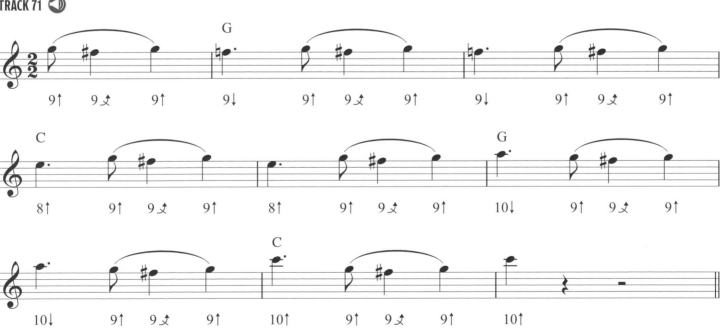

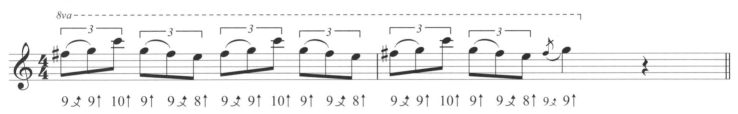

G

9↑   9↗   9↑   9↓   9↑   9↗   9↑   9↓   9↑   9↗   9↑

C

8↑   9↑   9↗   9↑   8↑   9↑   9↗   9↑   G 10↓   9↑   9↗   9↑

10↓   9↑   9↗   9↑   10↑   C 9↑   9↗   9↑   10↑

Here's a nice turnaround lick:

TRACK 72

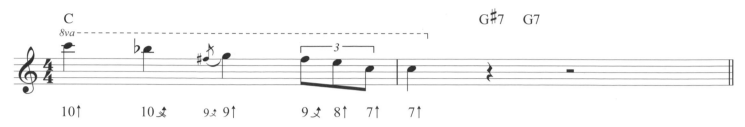

10↑   10⌣   9⌣ 9↑   9⌣ 8↑ 7↑   7↑

This lick also works well as a turnaround:

TRACK 73

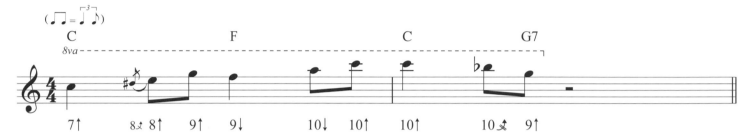

7↑   8⌣ 8↑ 9↑   9↓   10↓ 10↑   10↑   10⌣ 9↑

8-Hole Blow Bends

There's only one bend on the 8 hole. As with the 9 hole, it's possible to bend slightly past the half step, which creates an implied bend. Here's how the natural and bent notes sound:

TRACK 74

8↑   8⌣

This is how the 8-hole chromatic scale exercise sounds:

TRACK 75

8↑   8⌣   8↓   8⌣   8↑

Like the triplets on the 9 hole, there are some easy-to-play triplets that use the 8-hole bends. This first one starts on an 8-hole bend:

TRACK 76

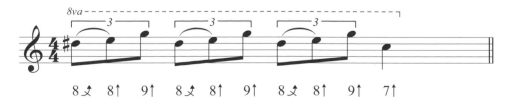

8⌣ 8↑ 9↑ 8⌣ 8↑ 9↑ 8⌣ 8↑ 9↑ 7↑

This next triplet starts on a natural 8-blow:

TRACK 77

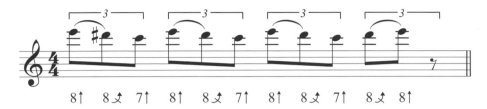

8↑ 8↗ 7↑   8↑ 8↗ 7↑   8↑ 8↗ 7↑   8↗ 8↑

This lick combines the previous two licks:

TRACK 78

8↗ 8↑ 9↑   8↑ 8↗ 7↑   8↗ 8↑ 9↑   8↑ 8↗ 7↑

Here's another sweet-sounding lick using 8-hole bends:

TRACK 79

8↑ 8↗ 8↑ 8↗   8↑ 9↑ 8↑ 8↗   8↑ 9↑ 8↑ 8↗ 7↑

A useful ascending lick like this one makes a good entrance into any solo. It is similar to the opening lick of Little Walter's "Juke":

TRACK 80

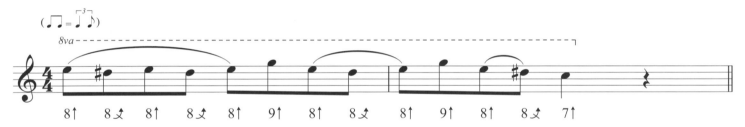

8↗ 8↑ 9↑ 10↓ 10↑ 10↑   8↗ 8↑ 9↑ 10↓ 10↑ 10↑

Here's a neat descending lick that uses a 10-hole bend and a 9-hole bend:

TRACK 81

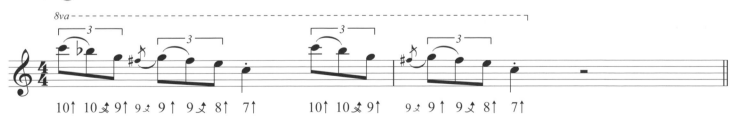

10↑ 10↗ 9↑ 9↗ 9↑ 9↗ 8↑ 7↑   10↑ 10↗ 9↑   9↗ 9↑ 9↗ 8↑ 7↑

The next example is similar to the previous one, except this time the lick ascends. It forces you to hit the second bend on 10 "cold" in the second triplet, as well as starting on the bent 9:

TRACK 82

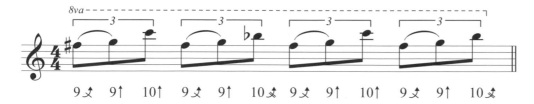

There are many ways to combine descending triplets. Take this lick for example:

TRACK 83

COLORING HIGH-NOTE BENDS

As with low-note bends, warbles and double stops can add coloring effects to your high-note and bent high-note playing. It is possible to achieve bent double stops on the 10-9, 9-8, and 8-7 combinations. Here they are:

TRACK 84 🔊

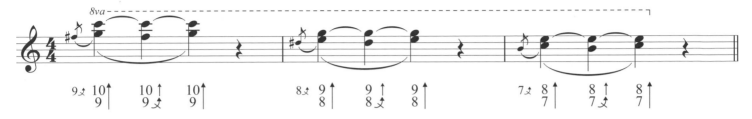

You can also bend high notes while executing high-note warbles:

TRACK 85 🔊

The following example is an improvised solo using some of the high-note techniques that have been presented:

TRACK 86 🔊   TRACK 86 PLAY ALONG 🔊

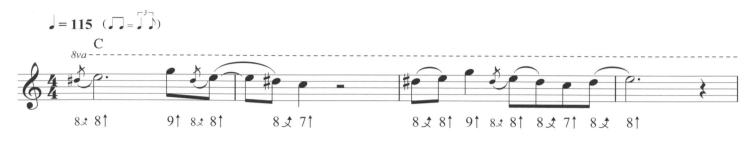

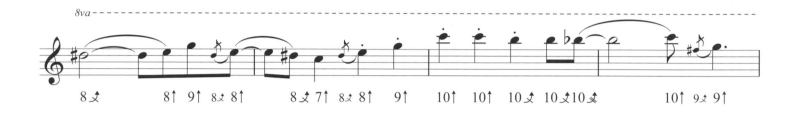

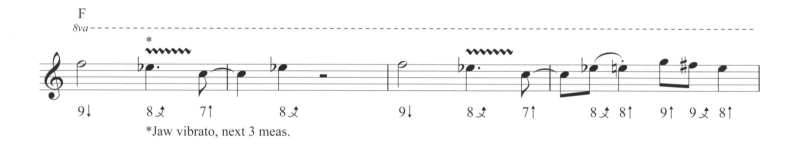

*Jaw vibrato, next 3 meas.

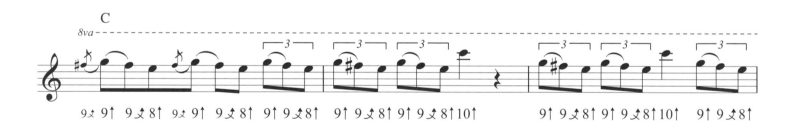

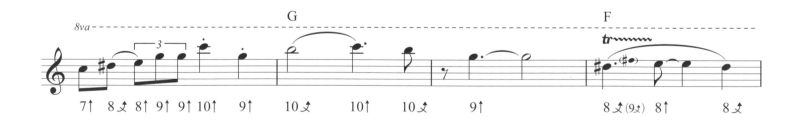

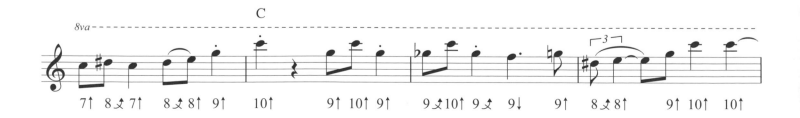

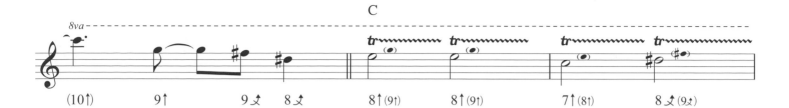

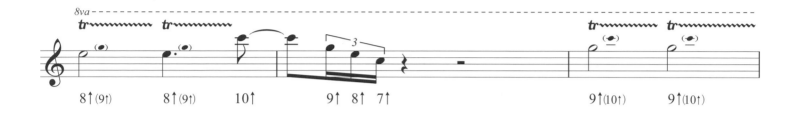

*Jaw vibrato

INTRODUCTION TO OVERBLOWING

In the early 1970s, another important innovation occurred. Credit must be given to pianist/harmonica player Howard Levy, who discovered a technique now called overblowing, by which all the notes of the chromatic scale could be achieved on the diatonic harmonica.

In note bending, the low- and mid-range notes of the harmonica are bent *down* while playing inhale notes. In overblowing, the lower- and mid-register notes are bent *up* while playing exhale notes.

In high-note bending, the bends are achieved while playing exhale notes and the notes are bent *down*.

Overblowing now provides us with the means to play the entire chromatic scale on the 10-hole diatonic harmonica. I feel that the discovery of the overblowing technique is as important to the advancement of the musical possibilities on the harmonica as the discovery of note bending was. In the four-plus decades since overblowing was discovered and incorporated, it too has become widely used by more and more harmonica players interested in playing the instrument in a way that can eliminate the traditional melodic limitations of the diatonic harmonica.

This section will focus on the three overblows in the middle register. That is enough to make it possible to play the whole chromatic scale in the middle register.

Achieving Overblow Notes

There are reasonably easy overblows on the 4, 5, and 6 holes that make it possible to play any melody. The 4-hole overblow raises the pitch 1-1/2 steps from the 4 blow, the 5 hole overblow raises the pitch by a whole step from the 5 blow, and the 6 hole overblows raise the pitch by 1-1/2 steps from the 6 blow. The embouchures are not unlike the configuration used when bending high notes while blowing. It's a little like trying to bend high notes, but in the middle register. This technique can be made easier by gapping the blow reeds on your harmonica a little wider than how they come from the factory. There are numerous tutorials available on YouTube on how to do this yourself, and there are also many competent harmonica technicians who can set your harps up for easier overblowing.

Overblowing in the Middle Register

As mentioned earlier, embouchures for overblowing are similar to high-note bending embouchures. At first, it may be helpful to start by bending some high notes. Then move down and try to apply that embouchure to the 6, 5, and 4 holes. When starting, it's easiest to free up the reed you want to overblow by first blowing the natural note, then drawing on that hole, and finally changing to a high note bending embouchure and digging in to overblow that hole. Like bending notes, it's a trial and error method of learning. You need to keep trying different embouchures until, eventually, an overblow will pop in for you. You may find that the overblow on the higher 6 hole is easier to achieve on a C harp than the lower 5 and 4 holes. One good strategy is to first bend the 7-hole blow note down (it is an implied bend that doesn't bend down an entire half step), then try using the same embouchure to try to overblow the 6 hole.

As with the bending exercises, once you can achieve an overblow, it's good training for your embouchure to hold that overblow as long as you can. This builds stamina and muscle memory. Unlike bending notes where you are bending through microtones, the overblown notes automatically play in tune.

Overblowing the 4 Hole

Here's how the 4-hole overblow sounds:

TRACK 87 🔊

The 4-hole overblow in sequence with the other notes on the 4 hole sounds like this:

TRACK 88

This tasty lick using the 4-hole overblow sounds great over a C minor chord:

TRACK 89

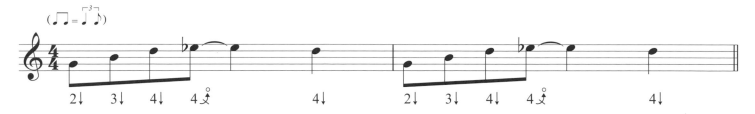

Starting with the G note that is 2 draw, this exercise includes the chromatic notes through E♭ (D♯), the 4 overblow. It incorporates the bends on 3 and 4 as well as the overblow on 4:

TRACK 90

Overblowing the 5 Hole

Here's how the 5-hole overblow sounds:

TRACK 91

Here's how the 5 overblow sounds in sequence with the other notes of the 5 hole:

TRACK 92

Yet another chromatic run begins on the 5 blow E note and ends on the 6 blow G note:

5↑   5↓   5↗̊   6↑

This next lick incorporates both the 4 and the 5 overblow and is transposed over the last four bars of a G blues progression:

TRACK 94

Our next example includes overblows on the 4 and 5 holes. Play this lick over a 12-bar blues progression in G:

TRACK 95   TRACK 95 PLAY ALONG

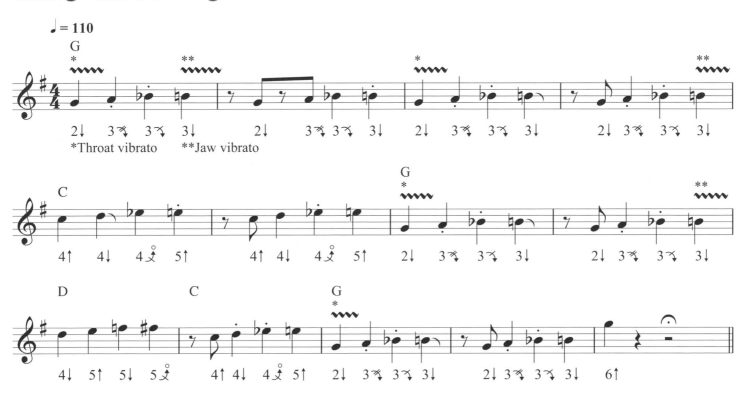

Overblowing the 6 Hole

Here's how the 6-hole overblow sounds:

TRACK 96

Here's how the 6-hole overblow sounds as a chromatic exercise:

TRACK 97

The chromatic notes on the 6 hole start with the 6-blow G note. This example continues through to the 7-blow C note:

TRACK 98

Now try a chromatic run starting with the 4-blow G note, through the 7-blow C note:

TRACK 99

And finally, let's move onto a chromatic run starting with the 2-blow E note, through the 7-blow C note:

TRACK 100

*Throat vibrato

Overblow Licks Over a 12-Bar Blues Progression in G

TRACK 101   TRACK 101 PLAY ALONG

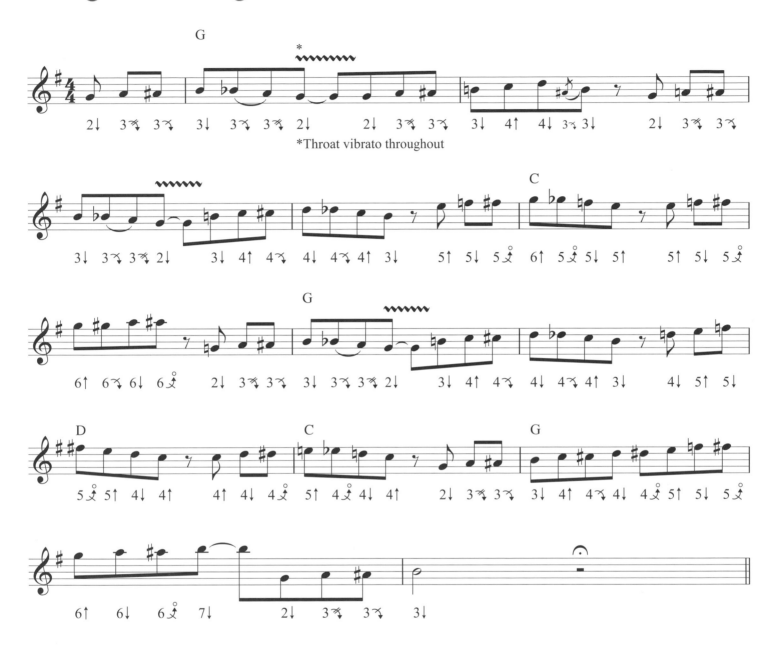

*Throat vibrato throughout

Our boogie woogie riff also works well in the middle and high registers:

TRACK 102 🔊 **TRACK 102 PLAY ALONG** 🔊

*Throat vibrato throughout

This next example features chromatic runs played over a 12-bar blues progression in G. The repeat signs tell you to play the first line twice:

TRACK 103   TRACK 103 PLAY ALONG

BRINGING IT ALL TOGETHER

This final section includes an overview of the techniques presented in this book, applied to 12-bar blues progressions in 1st, 2nd, and 3rd positions. These solos were improvised and are meant to demonstrate some possible ways to apply bends and ways of coloring natural and bent notes, double stops, and warbles over standard blues changes.

2nd Position, Key of G

TRACK 104  TRACK 104 PLAY ALONG

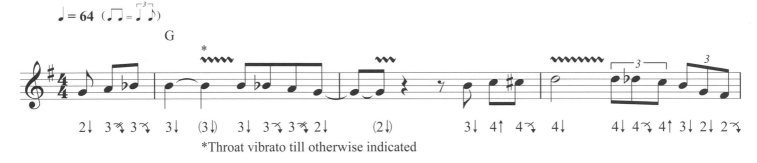

*Throat vibrato till otherwise indicated

**Ruffle
vibrato

*Throat vibrato, next 2 meas.

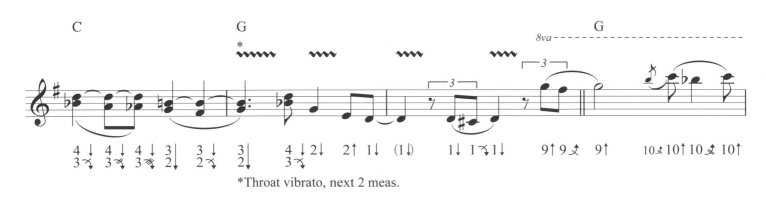

*Throat vibrato

3rd Position, Key of D

TRACK 105   TRACK 105 PLAY ALONG

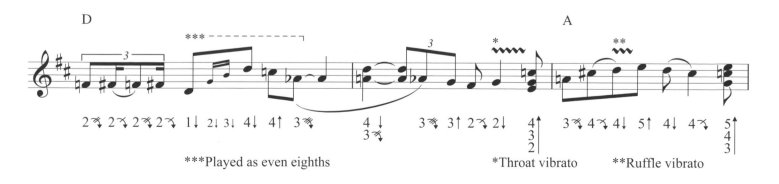

*Throat vibrato

**Ruffle vibrato

***Played as even eighths   *Throat vibrato   **Ruffle vibrato

*Throat vibrato

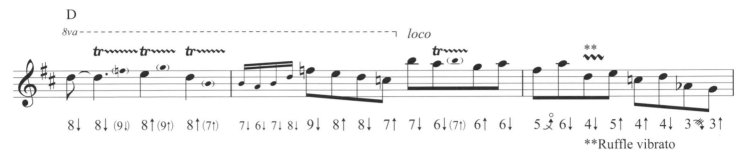

**Ruffle vibrato

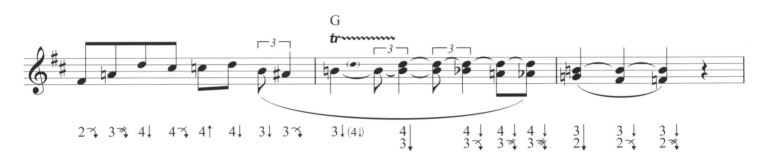

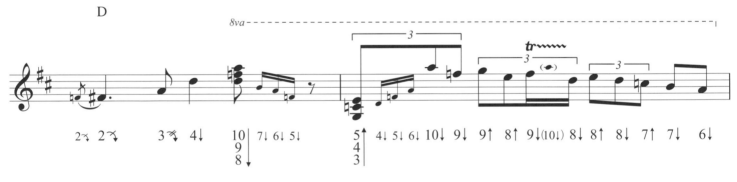

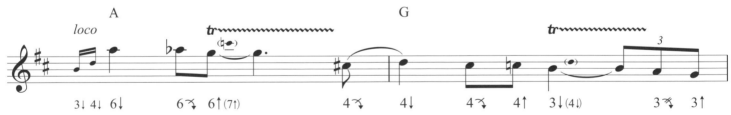

*Played as even eighths

1st Position, Key of C

*Throat vibrato till otherwise indicated

**Ruffle vibrato   *Throat vibrato

49

G

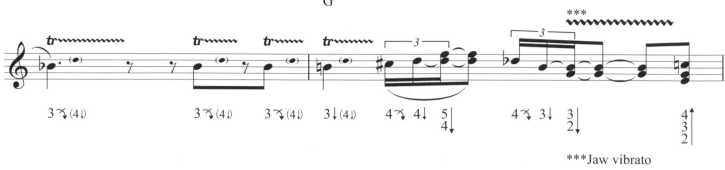

***Jaw vibrato

F   C

*Throat vibrato (both)

C HARP NOTE RECAP

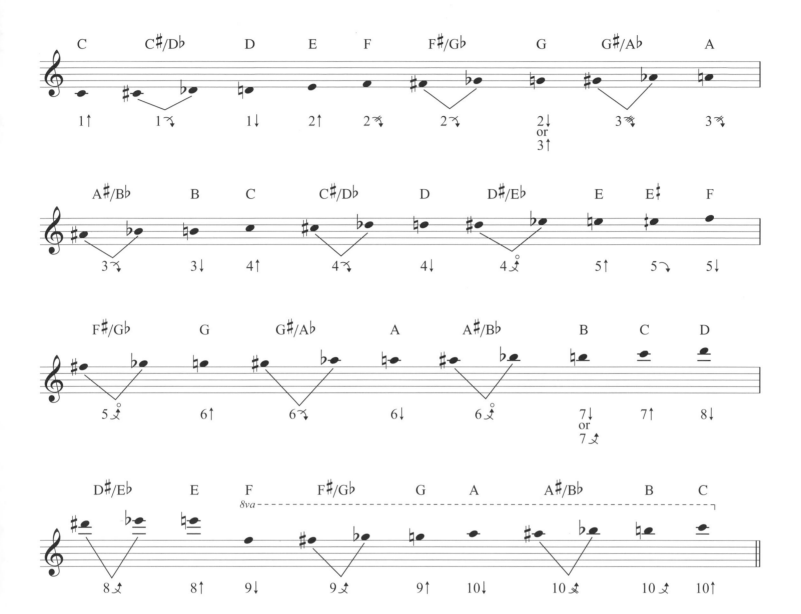

HARMONICA NOTATION LEGEND

Harmonica music can be notated two different ways: on a *musical staff*, and in *tablature*.

THE MUSICAL STAFF shows pitches and rhythms and is divided by bar lines into measures. Pitches are named after the first seven letters of the alphabet.

TABLATURE graphically represents the harmonica music. Each note will be accompanied by a number, 1 through 10, indicating what hole you are to play. The arrow that follows indicates whether to blow or draw. (All examples are shown using a C diatonic harmonica.)

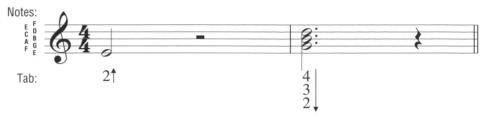

Blow (exhale) into 2nd hole.

Draw (inhale) 2nd, 3rd, & 4th holes together.

Notes on the C Harmonica

Exhaled (Blown) Notes

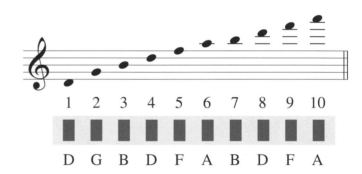

1 2 3 4 5 6 7 8 9 10

C E G C E G C E G C

Inhaled (Drawn) Notes

1 2 3 4 5 6 7 8 9 10

D G B D F A B D F A

Bends

Blow Bends

- 1/4 step
- 1/2 step
- 1 step
- 1 1/2 steps

Draw Bends

- 1/4 step
- 1/2 step
- 1 step
- 1 1/2 steps

Definitions for Special Harmonica Notation

SLURRED BEND: Play (draw) 3rd hole, then bend the note down one whole step.

GRACE NOTE BEND: Starting with a pre-bent note, immediately release bend to the target note.

VIBRATO: Begin adding vibrato to the sustained note on beat 3.

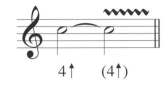

TONGUE BLOCKING: Using your tongue to block holes 2 & 3, play octaves on holes 1 & 4.

TRILL: Shake the harmonica rapidly to alternate between notes.

NOTE: Tablature numbers in parentheses are used when:

- The note is sustained, but a new articulation begins (such as vibrato), or
- The quantity of notes being sustained changes, or
- A change in dynamics (volume) occurs.
- It's the alternate note in a trill.

Additional Musical Definitions

D.S. al Coda

- Go back to the sign (𝄋), then play until the measure marked "***To Coda***," then skip to the section labelled "**Coda**."

D.C. al Fine

- Go back to the beginning of the song and play until the measure marked "***Fine***" (end).

- Repeat measures between signs.

   *(accent)*

- Accentuate the note (play initial attack louder).

   *(staccato)*

- Play the note short.

- When a repeated section has different endings, play the first ending only the first time and the second ending only the second time.

Dynamics

p   • Piano (soft)

mp   • Mezzo Piano (medium soft)

mf   • Mezzo Forte (medium loud)

f   • Forte (loud)

────────── *(crescendo)* • Gradually louder

────────── *(decrescendo)* • Gradually softer

HAL•LEONARD HARMONICA PLAY-ALONG

AUDIO ACCESS INCLUDED

Play your favorite songs quickly and easily!

Just follow the notation, listen to the audio to hear how the harmonica should sound, and then play along using the separate full-band backing tracks. The melody and lyrics are also included in the book in case you want to sing, or to simply help you follow along. The audio includes playback tools so you can adjust the recording to any tempo without changing pitch!

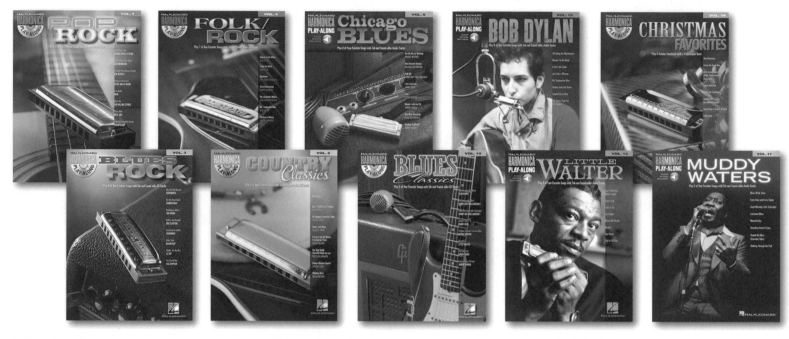

1. Pop/Rock
And When I Die • Bright Side of the Road • I Should Have Known Better • Low Rider • Miss You • Piano Man • Take the Long Way Home • You Don't Know How It Feels.
00000478...$15.99

2. Rock Hits
Cowboy • Hand in My Pocket • Karma Chameleon • Middle of the Road • Run Around • Smokin' in the Boys Room • Train in Vain • What I like About You.
00000479...$14.99

3. Blues/Rock
Big Ten Inch Record • On the Road Again • Roadhouse Blues • Rollin' and Tumblin' • Train Kept A-Rollin' • Train, Train • Waitin' for the Bus • You Shook Me.
00000481...$14.99

4. Folk/Rock
Blowin' in the Wind • Catch the Wind • Daydream • Eve of Destruction • Me and Bobby McGee • Mr. Tambourine Man • Pastures of Plenty.
00000482...$14.99

5. Country Classics
Blue Bayou • Don't Tell Me Your Troubles • He Stopped Loving Her Today • Honky Tonk Blues • If You've Got the Money (I've Got the Time) • The Only Daddy That Will Walk the Line • Orange Blossom Special • Whiskey River.
00001004...$14.99

6. Country Hits
Ain't Goin' down ('Til the Sun Comes Up) • Drive (For Daddy Gene) • Getcha Some • Here's a Quarter (Call Someone Who Cares) • Honkytonk U • One More Last Chance • Put Yourself in My Shoes • Turn It Loose.
00001013...$14.99

8. Pop Classics
Bluesette • Cherry Pink and Apple Blossom White • From Me to You • Love Me Do • Midnight Cowboy • Moon River • Peg O' My Heart • A Rainy Night in Georgia.
00001090...$14.99

9. Chicago Blues
Blues with a Feeling • Easy • Got My Mo Jo Working • Help Me • I Ain't Got You • Juke • Messin' with the Kid.
00001091...$14.99

10. Blues Classics
Baby, Scratch My Back • Eyesight to the Blind • Good Morning Little Schoolgirl • Honest I Do • I'm Your Hoochie Coochie Man • My Babe • Ride and Roll • Sweet Home Chicago.
00001093...$15.99

11. Christmas Carols
Angels We Have Heard on High • Away in a Manger • Deck the Hall • The First Noel • Go, Tell It on the Mountain • Jingle Bells • Joy to the World • O Little Town of Bethlehem.
00001296...$12.99

12. Bob Dylan
All Along the Watchtower • Blowin' in the Wind • It Ain't Me Babe • Just like a Woman • Mr. Tambourine Man • Shelter from the Storm • Tangled up in Blue • The Times They Are A-Changin'.
00001326 ....$16.99

13. Little Walter
Can't Hold Out Much Longer • Crazy Legs • I Got to Go • Last Night • Mean Old World • Rocker • Sad Hours • You're So Fine.
00001334...$14.99

14. Jazz Standards
Autumn Leaves • Georgia on My Mind • Lullaby of Birdland • Meditation (Meditacao) • My Funny Valentine • Satin Doll • Some Day My Prince Will Come • What a Wonderful World.
00001335...$16.99

15. Jazz Classics
All Blues • Au Privave • Comin' Home Baby •Song for My Father • Sugar • Sunny • Take Five • Work Song.
00001336 ....$14.99

16. Christmas Favorites
Blue Christmas • Frosty the Snow Man • Here Comes Santa Claus (Right down Santa Claus Lane) • Jingle-Bell Rock • Nuttin' for Christmas • Rudolph the Red-Nosed Reindeer • Santa Claus Is Comin' to Town • Silver Bells.
00001350...$14.99

17. Muddy Waters
Blow, Wind, Blow • Forty Days and Forty Nights • Good Morning Little Schoolgirl • Louisiana Blues • Mannish Boy • Standing Around Crying • Trouble No More (Someday Baby) • Walking Through the Park.
00821043 ....$14.99

HAL•LEONARD®
Visit Hal Leonard Online
at **www.halleonard.com**

Prices, content, and availability subject to change without notice.

THE HAL LEONARD HARMONICA
METHOD AND SONGBOOKS

THE METHOD

THE HAL LEONARD COMPLETE HARMONICA METHOD — CHROMATIC HARMONICA

by Bobby Joe Holman

The only harmonica method to present the chromatic harmonica in 14 scales and modes in all 12 keys! This book will take beginners from the basics on through to the most advanced techniques available for the contemporary harmonica player. Each section contains appropriate songs and exercises that enable the player to quickly learn the various concepts presented. Every aspect of this versatile musical instrument is explored and explained in easy-to-understand detail with illustrations. The musical styles covered include traditional, blues, pop and rock.

00841286 Book/Online Audio............................ $12.99

THE HAL LEONARD COMPLETE HARMONICA METHOD — DIATONIC HARMONICA

by Bobby Joe Holman

The only harmonica method specific to the diatonic harmonica, covering all six positions. This book/audio pack contains over 20 songs and musical examples that take beginners from the basics on through to the most advanced techniques available for the contemporary harmonica player. Each section contains appropriate songs and exercises (which are demonstrated through the online video) that enable the player to quickly learn the various concepts presented. Every aspect of this versatile musical instrument is explored and explained in easy-to-understand detail with illustrations. The musical styles covered include traditional, blues, pop and rock.

00841285 Book/Online Audio............................ $12.99

THE SONGBOOKS

The Hal Leonard Harmonica Songbook series offers a wide variety of music especially tailored to the two-volume Hal Leonard Harmonica Method, but can be played by all harmonica players, diatonic and chromatic alike. All books include study and performance notes, and a guide to harmonica tablature. From classical themes to Christmas music, rock and roll to Broadway, there's something for everyone!

BROADWAY SONGS FOR HARMONICA   INCLUDES TAB

arranged by Bobby Joe Holman

19 show-stopping Broadway tunes for the harmonica. Songs include: Ain't Misbehavin' • Bali Ha'i • Camelot • Climb Ev'ry Mountain • Do-Re-Mi • Edelweiss • Give My Regards to Broadway • Hello, Dolly! • I've Grown Accustomed to Her Face • The Impossible Dream (The Quest) • Memory • Oklahoma • People • and more.

00820009 ....$9.95

CLASSICAL FAVORITES FOR HARMONICA   INCLUDES TAB

arranged by Bobby Joe Holman

18 famous classical melodies and themes, arranged for diatonic and chromatic players. Includes: By the Beautiful Blue Danube • Clair De Lune • The Flight of the Bumble Bee • Gypsy Rondo • Moonlight Sonata • Surprise Symphony • The Swan (Le Cygne) • Waltz of the Flowers • and more, plus a guide to harmonica tablature.

00820006 ....$10.99

MOVIE FAVORITES FOR HARMONICA   INCLUDES TAB

arranged by Bobby Joe Holman

19 songs from the silver screen, arranged for diatonic and chromatic harmonica. Includes: Alfie • Bless the Beasts and Children • Chim Chim Cher-ee • The Entertainer • Georgy Girl • Midnight Cowboy • Moon River • Picnic • Speak Softly, Love • Stormy Weather • Tenderly • Unchained Melody • What a Wonderful World • and more, plus a guide to harmonica tablature.

00820014 ....$9.95

HAL•LEONARD®

Visit Hal Leonard Online at
www.halleonard.com

HAL•LEONARD

BLUES PLAY-ALONG

For use with all the C, B♭, Bass Clef and E♭ Instruments, the Hal Leonard Blues Play-Along Series is the ultimate jamming tool for all blues musicians.

With easy-to-read lead sheets, and other split-track choices, these first-of-a-kind packages will bring your local blues jam right into your house! Each song includes two tracks: a full stereo mix, and a split track mix with removable guitar, bass, piano, and harp parts. The CD is playable on any CD player, and is also enhanced so Mac and PC users can adjust the recording to any tempo without changing the pitch!

1. Chicago Blues
All Your Love (I Miss Loving) • Easy Baby • I Ain't Got You • I'm Your Hoochie Coochie Man • Killing Floor • Mary Had a Little Lamb • Messin' with the Kid • Sweet Home Chicago.
00843106 Book/CD Pack $15.99

2. Texas Blues
Hide Away • If You Love Me Like You Say • Mojo Hand • Okie Dokie Stomp • Pride and Joy • Reconsider Baby • T-Bone Shuffle • The Things That I Used to Do.
00843107 Book/CD Pack $12.99

3. Slow Blues
Don't Throw Your Love on Me So Strong • Five Long Years • I Can't Quit You Baby • I Just Want to Make Love to You • The Sky Is Crying • (They Call It) Stormy Monday (Stormy Monday Blues) • Sweet Little Angel • Texas Flood.
00843108 Book/CD Pack $12.99

4. Shuffle Blues
Beautician Blues • Bright Lights, Big City • Further on up the Road • I'm Tore Down • Juke • Let Me Love You Baby • Look at Little Sister • Rock Me Baby.
00843171 Book/CD Pack $12.99

5. B.B. King
Everyday I Have the Blues • It's My Own Fault Darlin' • Just Like a Woman • Please Accept My Love • Sweet Sixteen • The Thrill Is Gone • Why I Sing the Blues • You Upset Me Baby.
00843172 Book/CD Pack $14.99

7. Howlin' Wolf
Built for Comfort • Forty-Four • How Many More Years • Killing Floor • Moanin' at Midnight • Shake for Me • Sitting on Top of the World • Smokestack Lightning.
00843176 Book/CD Pack $12.99

8. Blues Classics
Baby, Please Don't Go • Boom Boom • Born Under a Bad Sign • Dust My Broom • How Long, How Long Blues • I Ain't Superstitious • It Hurts Me Too • My Babe.
00843177 Book/CD Pack $12.99

9. Albert Collins
Brick • Collins' Mix • Don't Lose Your Cool • Frost Bite • Frosty • I Ain't Drunk • Master Charge • Trash Talkin'.
00843178 Book/CD Pack $12.99

10. Uptempo Blues
Cross Road Blues (Crossroads) • Give Me Back My Wig • Got My Mo Jo Working • The House Is Rockin' • Paying the Cost to Be the Boss • Rollin' and Tumblin' • Turn on Your Love Light • You Can't Judge a Book by the Cover.
00843179 Book/CD Pack $12.99

11. Christmas Blues
Back Door Santa • Blue Christmas • Dig That Crazy Santa Claus • Merry Christmas, Baby • Please Come Home for Christmas • Santa Baby • Soulful Christmas.
00843203 Book/CD Pack $12.99

12. Jimmy Reed
Ain't That Lovin' You Baby • Baby, What You Want Me to Do • Big Boss Man • Bright Lights, Big City • Going to New York • Honest I Do • You Don't Have to Go • You Got Me Dizzy.
00843204 Book/CD Pack $12.99

13. Blues Standards
Ain't Nobody's Business • Kansas City • Key to the Highway • Let the Good Times Roll • Night Time Is the Right Time • Route 66 • See See Rider • Stormy Weather (Keeps Rainin' All the Time).
00843205 Book/CD Pack $12.99

14. Muddy Waters
Good Morning Little Schoolgirl • Honey Bee • I Can't Be Satisfied • I'm Ready • Mannish Boy • Rollin' Stone (Catfish Blues) • Trouble No More (Someday Baby) • You Shook Me.
00843206 Book/CD Pack $12.99

15. Blues Ballads
Ain't No Sunshine • As the Years Go Passing By • Darlin' You Know I Love You • Have You Ever Loved a Woman • I'd Rather Go Blind • Somebody Loan Me a Dime • Third Degree • Three Hours past Midnight.
00843207 Book/CD Pack $14.99

17. Stevie Ray Vaughan
Ain't Gone 'n' Give up on Love • Couldn't Stand the Weather • Crossfire • Empty Arms • Honey Bee • Love Struck Baby • Rude Mood • Scuttle Buttin'.
00843214 Book/Audio $14.99

18. Jimi Hendrix
Fire • Foxey Lady • Jam 292 • Little Wing • Red House • Spanish Castle Magic • Voodoo Child (Slight Return) • Who Knows.
00843218 Book/CD Pack $14.99

HAL•LEONARD®